Laura,
Happy Valentine's Day 1999
Love,
Mother

To live content with small means;
To seek elegance rather than luxury,
and refinement rather than fashion;
To be worthy, not respectable;
and wealthy, not rich;
To study hard,
think quietly,
talk gently,
act frankly;
To listen to stars and birds,
To babes and sages, with open heart,
to bear all cheerfully,
do all bravely,
await occasions,
hurry never.
...To let the spiritual, unbidden and unconscious,
grow up through the common.
This is to be my symphony.

MY SYMPHONY

BY
Wm. HENRY CHANNING

ILLUSTRATED BY
MARY ENGELBREIT

Andrews McMeel
Publishing

Kansas City

www.andrewsmcmeel.com

 is a registered trademark of Mary Engelbreit Enterprises, Inc.

ISBN: 0-8362-3674-2

Library of Congress Catalog Card Number: 97-73474

ATTENTION: SCHOOLS AND BUSINESSES

Andrews McMeel books are available at quantity discounts with bulk purchase for educational, business, or sales promotional use. For information, please write to: Special Sales Department, Andrews McMeel Publishing, 4520 Main Street, Kansas City, Missouri 64111.

for Evan
WITH LOVE

To live content
with small
means;

to
seek elegance
rather than
luxury,

And refinement rather than fashion;

to be WORTHY,

not respectable;

and WEALTHY, not rich;

To study hard,

Think
Quietly...

Talk Gently...

Act frankly;

To listen to stars

and birds,

To babes

and
Sages,

with
Open
Heart,

To bear all
Cheerfully,

do all bravely,

await occasions,

...To let the spiritual, unbidden and unconscious, grow up through the common.

This is to be my SYMPHONY.

ACKNOWLEDGMENTS

My heart  felt thanks to
Jean Lowe, Jackie Ahlstrom, and especially
the wonderful and wonderfully patient Wende Fink.
And to Phil for his understanding
and my sons for their inspiration.
And of course, to William Henry Channing
for penning such a wise poem.